LET'S GET SILLY!

Really Ridiculous Riddles

over 20 riddles!

BY CAITIE MCANENY

A-HA!

WHAT HAS HANDS, BUT CAN'T CLAP?

A CLOCK!

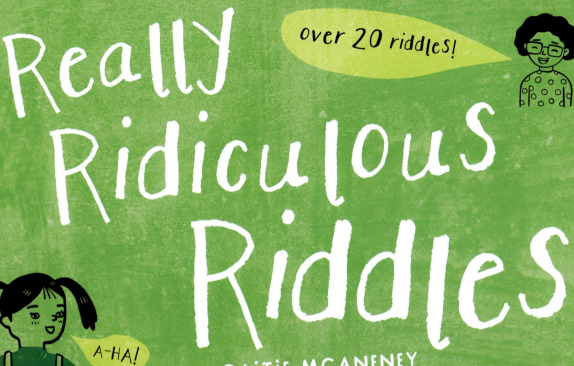

WINDMILL BOOKS

Published in 2025 by Windmill Books, an Imprint of Rosen Publishing
2544 Clinton St., Buffalo, NY 14224

Copyright © 2025 by The Rosen Publishing Group, Inc.

All rights reserved. No part of this book may be reproduced in any form without permission in writing from the publisher, except by a reviewer.

First Edition

Editor: Caitie McAneney
Book Design: Claire Zimmermann

Photo Credits: Series art (cover and interior illustrations) Huza Studio/Shutterstock.com; cover and interior (green painted background) elena_l/Shutterstock.com; cover, p. 1 (girl at top right corner) jesadaphorn/Shutterstock.com; series art (interior biege background paper) Q3kiaPictures/Shutterstock.com; p. 5 AI Generated/Shutterstock.com; p. 6 (comb) lineartestpilot/Shutterstock.com; p. 7 Sharomka/Shutterstock.com; p. 9 Kletr/Shutterstock.com; p. 11 Khosro/Shutterstock.com; p. 13 Arthur Balitskii/Shutterstock.com; p. 14 (goose) Polina Tomtosova/Shutterstock.com; p. 14 (zebra) IrinaOstapenko/Shutterstock.com; p. 15 Kevin White Photographer/Shutterstock.com; p. 17 Kuznetsov Dmitriy/Shutterstock.com; p. 18 (corn) Soffi/Shutterstock.com; p. 19 wavebreakmedia/Shutterstock.com; p. 21 MNStudio/Shutterstock.com.

Some of the images in this book illustrate individuals who are models. The depictions do not imply actual situations or events.

Library of Congress Cataloging-in-Publication Data

Names: McAneney, Caitie, author.
Title: Really ridiculous riddles / Caitie McAneney.
Description: Buffalo, NY : Windmill Books, 2025. | Series: Let's get silly! | Includes index.
Identifiers: LCCN 2024024844 (print) | LCCN 2024024845 (ebook) | ISBN 9781538397879 (library binding) | ISBN 9781538397862 (paperback) | ISBN 9781538397886 (ebook)
Subjects: LCSH: Riddles, Juvenile. | Wit and humor, Juvenile. | LCGFT: Riddles. | Humor.
Classification: LCC PN6371.5 .M387 2025 (print) | LCC PN6371.5 (ebook) | DDC 398.6-dc23/eng/20240626
LC record available at https://lccn.loc.gov/2024024844
LC ebook record available at https://lccn.loc.gov/2024024845

Manufactured in the United States of America

CPSIA Compliance Information: Batch #CWWM25. For further information, contact Rosen Publishing at 1-800-237-9932

Contents

What's a Riddle? 4
That's a Classic! 6
Heavy Hitters. 8
Great Delivery 10
Let's Look at Letters! 12
Guess the Animal 14
Body Language 16
Fun with Food 18
The Element of Surprise 20
Glossary 22
For More Information 23
Index 24

Words in the glossary appear in bold the first time they are used in the text.

What's a Riddle?

> What goes on four legs in the morning, two in the afternoon, and three in the evening?

In Greek mythology, the Sphinx would kill anyone who couldn't answer this riddle. The answer was "man," as he crawls, walks, and uses a cane as he gets older. Riddles
> Sphinx

are puzzling questions. They are often misleading. They really make you think!

That's a Classic!

WHAT IS TALL WHEN IT IS YOUNG AND SHORT WHEN IT IS OLD?
A candle.

WHAT IS A HOUSE THAT YOU ENTER BLIND BUT COME OUT SEEING?
A school.

I HAVE MANY TEETH BUT CAN'T BITE ANYTHING. WHAT AM I?
A hair comb.

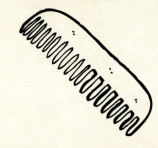

Fun Fact

The riddle of the house that teaches people to see is possibly the oldest riddle on Earth! It came from **ancient Sumer**—around 4,000 years ago.

Heavy Hitters

Ha!

What's easy to lift but hard to throw?
A feather.

What's as big as an elephant but weighs nothing?
Its shadow.

What weighs nothing but can't be held by even the strongest person on earth for 10 minutes?
Your breath.

Fun Fact
A male African elephant can weigh 15,000 pounds (6,804 kg)!

Great Delivery

WHAT TRAVELS THE WORLD BUT NEVER LEAVES ITS CORNER?
A stamp.

JOE'S MOM SENDS A LETTER TO EACH OF HER SONS—SNAP, CRACKLE, AND ____.
Joe.

WHAT HAS ONLY ONE LETTER, BUT BEGINS AND ENDS WITH E?
An envelope.

Fun Fact

The first **adhesive** stamp was used in 1840 in the United Kingdom.

Let's Look at Letters!
E F G

WHAT IS FOUND TWICE IN A STATE, BUT ONLY ONCE IN THE WHOLE COUNTRY?
The letter T.

WHAT IS FOUND ONCE IN A MINUTE AND TWICE IN A MOMENT, BUT NEVER IN A THOUSAND YEARS?
The letter M.

LOL!

WHAT APPEARS IN MERCURY, EARTH, MARS, AND JUPITER, BUT NEVER VENUS?
The letter R.

:*. Fun Fact *

Except for Earth, every planet in our **solar system** was named after Greek and Roman gods.

13

Guess the Animal

AS I GROW UP, I GROW DOWN. WHAT AM I?
A goose.

I SIT WHEN I STAND AND JUMP WHEN I WALK. WHAT AM I?
A kangaroo.

WHILE THE ALPHABET GOES FROM A TO Z, I GO FROM Z TO A. WHAT AM I?
A zebra.

Fun Fact

Geese have a soft, fluffy layer of feathers underneath their topcoat. This layer, called down, keeps them dry and warm.

Body Language

WHAT HAS ARMS BUT NO HANDS AND A NECK BUT NO HEAD?
A shirt.

IT CAN RUN BUT CAN'T WALK. WHAT IS IT?
A nose.

THE MORE OF THESE YOU MAKE, THE MORE YOU LEAVE BEHIND YOU.
Footsteps.

Fun Fact

The average American takes around 4,000 steps a day.

17

Fun with Food

WHAT **STALKS** A FARM WITH EARS THAT NEVER HEAR? Corn.

WHAT IS USED ONLY AFTER IT'S BROKEN? An egg.

WHAT IS COVERED IN EYES, BUT IS TOTALLY BLIND? A potato.

HEEHEE!

18

Fun Fact

About one in every 1,000 eggs has a double YOLK!

19

The Element of Surprise

WHAT CAN BE MADE BUT NOT SEEN OR HELD?
Noise.

FEED IT, AND IT GROWS. GIVE IT WATER, AND IT DIES. WHAT IS IT?
Fire.

WHAT TAKES UP NO SPACE, BUT CAN FILL A ROOM?
Light.

HAHA!

Fun Fact

The four **elements** in nature are fire, water, air, and earth.

Glossary

adhesive: Able to stick to something.

ancient: From a long time ago.

element: A basic part of something.

mythology: A collection of myths, or stories, passed down from a certain group of people.

solar system: Any system that includes a star and all of the matter that orbits that star, including planets and moons.

Sphinx: A mythical creature with the body of a lion, wings of an eagle, and head of a human.

stalk: A plant's main stem; also, to follow in a way that's like hunting.

yolk: The yellow part of an egg.

For More Information

BOOKS

Huddleston, Emma. *Animal Riddles*. Mankato, MN: The Child's World, 2022.

King, Joe. *Rad Riddles*. Minneapolis, MN: Abdo Kids Junior, 2024.

Watts, Mandisa. *The Big Riddle Book for Kids*. Oakland, CA: Rockridge Press, 2022.

WEBSITES

Riddles
www.ducksters.com/jokes/riddles.php
Discover more entertaining riddles with Ducksters.

What Am I?
kids.nationalgeographic.com/videos/topic/what-am-i
See if you can use your riddle skills to guess which animal each video is about.

Index

alphabet, 14
country, 12
eggs, 18, 19
elements, 21
elephant, 8, 9
farm, 18
geese, 14, 15
Greek gods, 13
Greek mythology, 4

letters, 10, 12
Roman gods, 13
school, 6
solar system, 13
Sphinx, 4
stamps, 10, 11
Sumer, 7
United Kingdom, 11
weight, 8, 9